Animal Opposites

HIGH

and

LOW

An Animal Opposites Book

by Nathan Olson

Capstone
press

Mankato, Minnesota

Some animals hang from high cave ceilings.
Other animals live low in colonies underground.

Let's learn about high and low by looking at animals around the world.

HIGH

Pandas climb high in trees. They also munch bamboo most of the day.

LOW

Brown bears hunt down low for food.
They eat wild berries and salmon.

HIGH

Tree squirrels scamper high up in trees to build their nests.

Ground squirrels dig down low to make their homes in the ground.

LOW

HIGH

Eagles fly high to build nests on the tops of tall trees.

Many eagles come back to the same nest each year.

8

LOW

Sea turtles lay their eggs down low in a sandy hole.

9

HIGH

Mountain goats make their homes up high. They live on steep mountain ledges.

LOW

Goatfish live low on the ocean floor. They wiggle their whiskers to find food hidden in the sand.

Goatfish can change colors to blend in with their surroundings.

HIGH

Spotted leopards rest up high. They sit on tree branches and watch for prey to come near.

LOW

Lions snooze down low in the grass. They sometimes sleep 20 hours a day.

HIGH

Red-eyed tree frogs use their sticky feet to climb high on rain forest plants.

LOW

Bullfrogs hide low in the water.
They look for tasty bugs to eat.

HIGH

Colonies of fruit bats sleep up high. They hang upside down from cave ceilings.

Families of prairie dogs dig down low.
They live in colonies underground.

HIGH

Oak treehoppers are insects
that live high on oak trees.

LOW

Ground beetles live
low on the ground.
They hide under rocks
and leaves to stay safe.

19

HIGH

Playful dolphins jump up high out of the water.

Dolphins use clicks and whistles to talk to each other.

LOW

They also dive down low to see what is on the ocean floor.

HIGH

Giraffes stretch
to eat leaves
up high in the trees.

Aardvarks stick their snouts down low.
They eat ants and termites underground.

Aardvarks can eat 50,000 insects in one night. They lick them up with their long tongues.

23

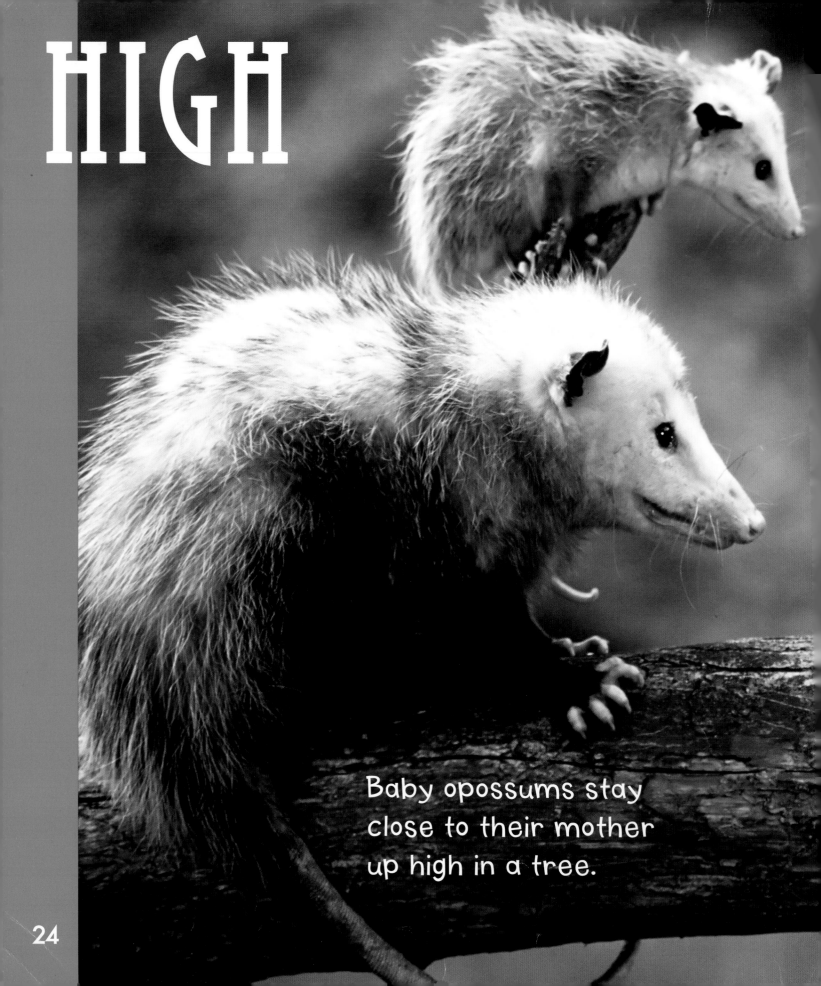

HIGH

Baby opossums stay
close to their mother
up high in a tree.

24

LOW

Warthog piglets stay close to their mother down low on the ground.

When warthogs run, they wave their tails in the air like flags.

Some animals climb high to find food.
Others live low on the ocean floor.

What kinds of high and low animals live near you?

Did You Know?

Sea turtles spend their whole lives in the water. Females return to land only to lay their eggs. Most males never return to land.

Red-eyed tree frogs sleep during the day. They close their eyes to blend in with the green surroundings. If an enemy wakes them up, their red eyes scare it away.

Adult pandas eat for about 10 to 16 hours a day. They eat anywhere from 20 to 80 pounds (9 to 36 kilograms) of bamboo in a single day.

Eagles add to their nests each year. Some eagle nests become very big and heavy. They can weigh as much as a hippopotamus.

The Congress Avenue Bridge in Austin, Texas, is home to 1.5 million bats. They eat at least 10,000 pounds (4,536 kilograms) of insects each night.

Glossary

bamboo (bam-BOO) — a tropical plant with a hard, hollow stem

colony (KOL-uh-nee) — a large group of animals that live together

enemy (EN-uh-mee) — a person or animal that wants to harm or destroy another

prey (PRAY) — an animal that is hunted by another animal for food

rain forest (RAYN FOR-ist) — a thick forest where a great deal of rain falls

salmon (SAM-uhn) — a large fish with silvery skin

scamper (SKAM-pur) — to run lightly and quickly

snout (SNOUT) — the long front part of an animal's head that includes the nose, mouth, and jaws

surroundings (suh-ROUN-dingz) — the things around something or someone

termite (TUR-mite) — an antlike insect that eats wood

Read More

Bullard, Lisa. *Fast and Slow: An Animal Opposites Book*. A+ Books: Animal Opposites. Mankato, Minn.: Capstone Press, 2006.

Seeger, Laura Vaccaro. *Black? White! Day? Night!: A Book of Opposites*. New Milford, Conn.: Roaring Brook Press, 2006.

Shulman, Mark. *Opposites: Big Bagel, Little Bagel*. Bagel Books. New York: Grosset & Dunlap, 2003.

Internet Sites

FactHound offers a safe, fun way to find Internet sites related to this book. All of the sites on FactHound have been researched by our staff.

Here's how:

1. Visit *www.facthound.com*

2. Choose your grade level.

3. Type in this book ID **1429612118** for age-appropriate sites. You may also browse subjects by clicking on letters, or by clicking on pictures and words.

4. Click on the **Fetch It** button.

FactHound will fetch the best sites for you!

Index

A+ Books are published by Capstone Press,
151 Good Counsel Drive, P.O. Box 669, Mankato, Minnesota 56002.
www.capstonepress.com

1 2 3 4 5 6 13 12 11 10 09 08

Library of Congress Cataloging-in-Publication Data
Olson, Nathan.
  High and low: an animal opposites book / by Nathan Olson.
    p. cm. — (A+ books. Animal opposites)
  Includes bibliographical references and index.
  ISBN-13: 978-1-4296-1211-1 (hardcover)
  ISBN-10: 1-4296-1211-8 (hardcover)
    1. Animal behavior — Juvenile literature. 2. Animals — Habitations — Juvenile literature.
I. Title. II. Series.
QL751.5.O47 2008
591.5 — dc22   2007036218

Summary: Brief text introduces the concepts of high and low, comparing some of the world's
    highest and lowest animals.

Credits
Heather Adamson and Megan Peterson, editors; Renée T. Doyle, designer;
    Wanda Winch, photo researcher

Photo Credits
Art Life Images/age fotostock/Bartomeu Borrell, 19; Art Life Images/age fotostock/Nigel
Dennis, 23; Bat Conservation International/Dr. Merlin D. Tuttle, 16; Comstock Images, 28;
Creatas, 26 (top), 27 (top); Getty Images Inc./Gallo Images/Heinrich van den Berg, 25 (top
right); Getty Images Inc./Minden Pictures/Michael Quinton, 8; Getty Images Inc./Visuals
Unlimited/Steve Maslowski, 24–25; iStockphoto/Justin Horrocks, 27 (middle); iStockphoto/
Sebastian Duda, 14; iStockphoto/Tomasz Resiak, 3 (bottom); Jupiter Images/Corbis, 4;
Peter Arnold/Malcolm Schuyl, 7; SeaPics.com/Doug Perrine, cover (goatfish), 11;
Shutterstock/Baloncici, 2 (bottom); Shutterstock/Bill Kennedy, 15; Shutterstock/EcoPrint, 13,
27 (bottom); Shutterstock/Eric Isselee, 3 (middle right); Shutterstock/Igor Shootov, cover
(mountain goat); Shutterstock/Jonathan Larsen, 17; Shutterstock/Ke Wang, 1 (middle), 2
(top); Shutterstock/Kristian Sekulic, 20; Shutterstock/L.S. Luecke, 1 (right), 26 (bottom);
Shutterstock/Peter Kunasz, 10–11; Shutterstock/Rick Parsons, 5; Shutterstock/Rick
Thornton, 6; Shutterstock/Sean Nel, 22; Shutterstock/Stuart Taylor, 12; Shutterstock/Tom C.
Amon, 1 (left), 3 (top); Shutterstock/Tom Hirtreiter, 21; SuperStock, Inc./age fotostock, 9;
USDA Forest Service/Bugwood.org/Larry R. Barber, 18

Note to Parents, Teachers, and Librarians
This Animal Opposites book uses full-color photographs and a nonfiction format to
introduce children to the concepts of high and low. *High and Low* is designed to be
read aloud to a pre-reader or to be read independently by an early reader.
Photographs help listeners and early readers understand the text and concepts
discussed. The book encourages further learning by including the following
sections: Did You Know?, Glossary, Read More, Internet Sites, and Index. Early
readers may need assistance using these features.